THE SONG OF CREATION

The Story of Genesis

Michael Sharp

www.michaelsharp.org

Avatar Publications

http://www.avatarpublication.com/

Published by

Avatar Publications™

www.avatarpublication.com

Copyright 2005 by Michael Sharp ©

All Rights Reserved

This book printed on acid free paper.

ISBN 978-0-9737401-6-5 (Paper)
ISBN 978-0-9737401-7-2 (PDF eBook)

All art work copyright Nicole Mocellin©
nicole.mocellin@wanadoo.fr

For information on bulk purchase discounts contact
Avatar Publications at sales@avatarpublication.com

Library of Congress Cataloging-in-Publication Data

Sharp, Michael, 1963-
    The song of creation : the story of Genesis / Michael Sharp.
        p. cm.
    ISBN 978-0-9737401-6-5 (alk. paper) -- ISBN 978-0-9737401-7-2 (pdf)
1. Creation--Miscellanea. 2. Cosmology--Miscellanea. I. Title.

BF1999.S439 2007
  202'.4--dc22

                                                      2007006923

The eBook of the *Song of Creation* is available for free
non-commercial distribution from
http://www.michaelsharp.org/

For commercial rights, contact sales@avatarpublication.com

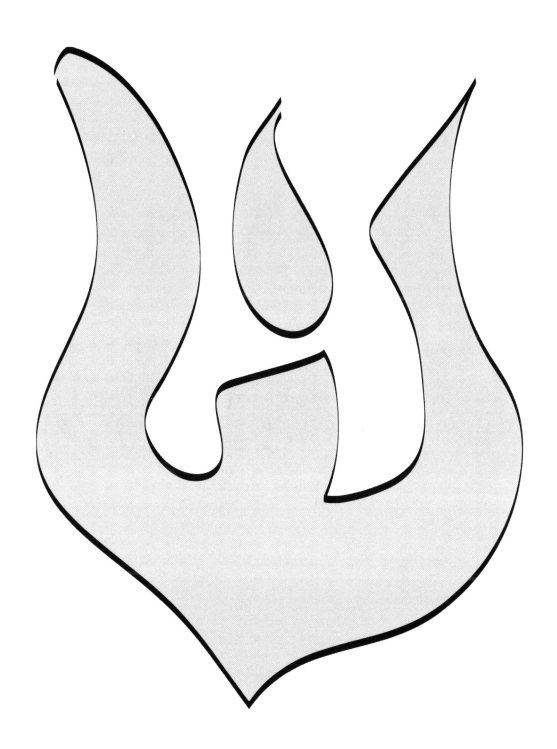

Joy is a net of love by which you can catch souls

Mother Teresa

Your vision will become clear only
when you look into your heart...
Who looks outside, dreams.
Who looks inside, awakens.

Carl Jung

Part One

Dance of the Star

In the beginning

Spirit was and Spirit moved.

Alpha and omega.

Beginning without end.

No thing and everything contained in one **unlimited, unrealized** potential.

And then, *Spirit thought.*

And from that thought sprang **all of creation**.

As Spirit thought, creation responded.

Shapes and colors and sounds emerged to delight and bring glory to Spirit.

And Spirit wanted for nothing, for whatever Spirit wanted was instantly manifest in creation.

Spirit danced and played and grew in power and knowledge over creation.

But then, a time came when Spirit had mastered the intricate art of creation and exhausted the potentials of imagination.

And so, Spirit thought.

Spirit had created infinite wonder and beauty. Shapes and forms, colors and configurations had danced in the awareness of Spirit.

And yet, for all the awesome power of Spirit, creation was transient and ephemeral.

The energy was too hot and the form too fleeting.

And so, Spirit thought. What wonder would there be if all things that delighted and stretched the imagination would last?

So Spirit thought and from that thought the energies were reduced, the vibration slowed and, with a great explosion of light and love, a new universe was born.

As Spirit had intended, things were different at this level.

As the vibration slowed and the fires cooled, creation became thick and physicality became dark.

Now, Spirit required time to create.

Still, Spirit thought and from the thought of Spirit did spring crystal palaces and lush gardens, beautiful music and exalted art.

From the thought of Spirit did spring many wondrous forms as vehicles for the magnificence of Spirit.

Blue Landscape

And Spirit wanted for nothing, for Spirit was alpha and omega, beginning without end and whatever Spirit wanted was instantly manifest and the whole of creation proved a wondrous playground for Spirit.

But when Spirit had mastered the intricacies of creation and exhausted the potentials of imagination, Spirit thought.

Spirit had created infinite wonder and beauty and had experienced infinite variety and delight, but the effects were transient, the creation ephemeral, the energy too hot.

Spirit wondered.

What marvel would there be if the creations of Spirit could last?

And so, Spirit thought and from that thought the energies were reduced, the vibration slowed and, with a great explosion of light and love, a new universe was born.

As Spirit had intended, things were different at this level, for as the energy was reduced and the vibration slowed, creation became thick and dark, viscous and slow.

In these new conditions, Spirit required more time to create.

But now, creation lasted longer and Spirit drew much delight from the interaction of form and time.

And Spirit thought and from that thought did spring crystal palaces and lush gardens, beautiful music and exalted art and Spirit wanted for nothing for Spirit was alpha and omega, beginning without end, and whatever Spirit wanted was instantly manifest and the whole of creation proved a wondrous playground for Spirit.

But when Spirit had mastered the intricacies of creation and exhausted the potential of imagination, Spirit wanted more.

Despite the awesome power and the glory of the universe, Spirit stood outside as a thing apart from creation.

Spirit could see, but could not experience.

Spirit could hear, but could not *feel*.

So Spirit thought.

And as our thought spread out over the darkness,

And as our breath spread out over the waters,

And as our hand reached down into the fires,

Life sprang forth.

No pessimist ever discovered the secrets of the stars,
or sailed to an unchartered lands,
or opened a new heaven to the human spirit.

Helen Keller

Part Two

Fallen from the Sky

As Spirit had intended, things were different in this world. Now, Spirit would work *from within* the created universe.

And Spirit thought and from the thought of Spirit sprang the trees and the plants, the fish and the birds, the creatures and all the vehicles of Spirit.

And as each new vehicle evolved on the planets in the universe, the eyes of The Body of Spirit gazed upon the wonders of creation.

There were crystal palaces and lush gardens, beautiful music and exalted art. Great political forms expressed the perfection of Spirit and great economic forms spread the prosperity of Spirit.

Creation unfolded and light poured into the universe and yet for all the splendor and magnificence of the life of The Body, still there were limitations.

This new creation, these fragile forms of life, these glittering vehicles of Spirit, this Body of our Christ, was delicate and easily damaged.

Victim of the smallest insult and troubled by the slightest imbalance, the body was frail.

Twisted by the slightest negativity and damaged by the absence of Love, the mind was weak and in its weak and fragile state the body/mind could not contain the full glory of Spirit.

For consciousness was fire and the molecules of the universe cold like ice.

The Spirit was willing, but the flesh was weak.

But the flesh could be made strong.

So Spirit danced in the love and prosperity of creation and as Spirit danced, The Body evolved and the mind strengthened.

The fish in the sea and the birds in the air, the beasts on the land and the worms in the garden, the black, the white, the red, and the yellow became wonderful vehicles for the experience of creation.

Soon it was thought, The Body would be the perfect vehicle and the mind the perfect lens and Spirit would enter without limitation, for surely in this entire physical universe, which was in the imagination of Spirit, there can be no limitation.

But eventually a point in the development of The Body was reached.

The Body would no longer evolve.

The mind would no longer strengthen.

And Spirit understood that at this dense level of creation, the full glory of Spirit would **never** be able to enter The Body.

The molecules were too fragile. The fires too hot.

So Spirit thought.

Moor and Heather

And Spirit thought.

And Spirit understood that only by *lifting* creation would the full power of Spirit (which is God, as **you** know) be able to enter.

And so Spirit thought.

The universe would return to the fires.

The universe would ascend in vibration.

The universe would have to come home.

And so, Spirit thought and from that thought light spread out over the waters and a new world was born.

And Spirit thought.

In this new world, Spirit would stoke the fires of creation and bring heat to the cold molecules of physicality.

It would not be easy, but it would be done.

So Spirit thought and in this new world and in those hearts of yours, **duality** was increased.

Day passed into night.

The seasons cycled in opposition.

Black opposed white and The Body struggled in duality for Spirit understood that in struggle and opposition great energy would be created.

The bodies would fight, the bodies would feel and in the struggle and the feeling the bodies would light the molecules and lift the universe.

And so Spirit thought and on this planet and with this form, *Lemuria* unfolded.

There were crystal palaces and lush gardens, beautiful music and exalted art.

There were political forms that expressed the perfection of Spirit and equitable economies where flowed the prosperity of God.

Duality spread across this world and energy poured forth from The Body.

And Spirit struggled long and hard in the duality of this earth, but no matter how hard the struggle, not enough energy could be created.

The universe remained at a distance and the molecules remained cold.

The duality was not enough for no matter how Spirit struggled, and no matter how Spirit fought, The Body remembered the unity of Spirit.

Stardust

The Body remembered the Love of creation.

The Body remembered the illusion of duality.

And though it was true that in opposition our bodies struggled,

And though it was true that in duality we fought,

In awareness and oneness our Spirit rejoiced.

We laughed at the struggle and duality.

How could we not?

We understood it was illusion and that in truth we are one.

And in the joy and the laughter at the great joke of duality, the energy was dissipated and the ascension would not proceed.

So Spirit thought.

If the energy could not be created, **The Great Work** would not be accomplished.

So Spirit thought.

And Spirit thought.

And Spirit thought.

And finally, Spirit realized.

In order to live in duality, in order that all might believe, the mind must be covered in darkness.

The Body would have to forget!

Exhilarated by the beauty of *The Plan*, Spirit thought and from that thought **The Veil** was created.

And Spirit thought.

And The Body fell into amnesia.

Beneath The Veil, The Body struggled.

Beneath The Veil, The Body cried.

Beneath The Veil, The Body died.

The Veil was thick.

The Veil was strong.

Flood of Fire

The Veil hid us from Spirit.

The Veil darkened the mind.

The Veil blurred us from Source.

But beneath The Veil, duality *crackled*.

Beneath The Veil, *Atlantis* was born.

And in Atlantis **The Body thought**.

And on this planet and with this form, The Body created wonders.

There were palaces and gardens, music and art.

There were political forms that expressed a shadow of the glory.

There were economic systems that obscured the prosperity of creation.

Duality raged across the face of the earth and the energy crackled.

Day passed into night.

The seasons cycled in opposition.

Black opposed white and The Body struggled with emotion.

For Spirit understood that in struggle and opposition great energy was created.

The bodies fought.

The bodies felt.

The bodies radiated.

And The Body proceeded towards ascension.

After a certain period of time, a point was reached.

The energy was sufficient.

The Ascension would proceed!

So in great excitement, Spirit sent out a call to the bodies beneath The Veil.

NOW IS THE TIME to awake, cried Spirit.

NOW IS THE TIME to be free!

Fault of Fire

NOW IS THE TIME TO REMEMBER.

The energy is sufficient.

The Ascension will proceed.

But The Body could not hear **The Call** of its Spirit.

The Veil was too thick.

The Body cut off.

So Spirit thought and from that thought a call went out and only the **most devoted** responded for only the most devoted could find their way back through The Veil.

And Spirit thought and from that thought the **Messengers** fell into darkness.

They struggled to awaken.

They opened their eyes.

They remembered and they said to the sleepers around them,

"We are One."

"We are Joy."

"We are Love."

"We are GOD!"

But the sleepers did not awake.

The Body had forgotten.

The Body was deaf.

The Body knew only survival.

The Body knew only its death.

The Body doubted the message and scoffed at the messengers.

Instead of the unity of Spirit, The Body felt separation of ego.

Instead of the joy of creation, The Body felt sorrow at limitation.

Instead of the love of creators, The Body felt anger and isolation.

And out of the separation and sorrow, anger and rage, The Body lashed out.

The Body struck back and The Body learned fear.

And from the anger and pain, from the fear and the sorrow, a terrible darkness spread over the land.

Rose

The strong trampled the weak.

And the darkness grew.

The rich exploited the poor.

And the darkness grew.

The healthy murdered the sick.

And the darkness grew.

Till Spirit cried, "This must not be."

The pain is too great.

This must not be!

And from the cry of our Spirit, the civilization of Atlantis died.

And that part of Spirit not trapped in **The Wheel** wept at the loss.

And from that weeping a new world, **our world**, was born.

Anyone who claims to be to be in the light
but hates his brother is still in the dark.

1 John 2:9

Part Three

Temple Keepers

As Spirit had intended, things were different in this world.

In this world, as in the one before, The Body would exist in duality and play in the darkness.

For Spirit understood that in struggle and opposition great energy was created.

But now Spirit also understood that the darkness of The Veil and the great power of the Body would lead unto death if unchecked and unguarded.

This, Spirit could not allow.

Thus, until the energy was sufficient **and** the Body would remember, we would be kept tight in bondage.

We would be kept from our power.

So Spirit thought, and as the new world unfolded, Spirit sent a call out to the omniverse and only the **most loving** responded for only they would bind us in fear.

And Spirit thought and from that thought the most loving, now the **Forces of Darkness**, fell into amnesia.

And they bound us with fear.

And they made slaves of our bodies.

And they chained fast our minds.

And they kept us from power.

And Spirit watched, and the Body thought.

And as the Body thought, **Terra** unfolded and there were palaces and gardens, music and art.

There were political forms that expressed the limitations of our energy.

There were economies that reduced the flow in the system.

Duality raged across the face of this world.

Poverty swept the land.

Darkness enveloped our minds.

Death took hold of our souls.

The seasons cycled in opposition.

Day passed into night.

The bodies fought.

The bodies felt.

The bodies radiated.

White Flower

And the Body proceeded towards ascension.

Now, after a certain period of time, a point was reached.

The energy was sufficient and the ascension would proceed.

So in great excitement Spirit sent out a call to the bodies.

NOW IS THE TIME to awake, cried our Spirit.

NOW IS THE TIME to remember.

NOW IS THE TIME to be free!

The energy is sufficient.

The Ascension will proceed.

But the Body could not hear The Call.

The Body was dead to the glory.

The Body had forgotten.

The Body was deaf.

And so Spirit sent a call and the messengers returned and they descended into darkness.

And they opened their eyes.

And they remembered.

And they said to the sleepers around them,

"We are one."

"We are Joy."

"We are Love."

"We are GOD!"

But the Body knew only survival.

The Body knew only its death.

The Body doubted the messengers and grew angry at isolation.

But it did not matter.

The Dark Forces kept us from power.

Tormented Sky

The Dark Forces prevented collapse.

So the messengers taught of Love and Compassion, the Unity of Spirit, and the source of all Love.

And some listened, but others did not.

The messengers spoke of energy and light and the nature of creation.

And some listened, but others did not.

But as time passed and the messengers persisted, more came to recall.

And when enough had remembered the love in creation, the bonds could be loosed and the energy freed.

And so Spirit thought.

And Spirit called.

And only the **most compassionate** responded for only they could free us from fear.

And Spirit thought and from that thought the **Lightseeds** fell into darkness.

And Spirit watched.

And the Lightseeds awoke.

And the Lightseeds asked of the Body, "Are we one?"

And the Body replied "Yes."

And the Lightseeds asked "Are we joy?"

And the Body replied "Yes."

And the Lightseeds asked "Are we God?"

And the Body replied "Yes."

And seeing that the way was prepared, the Lightseeds said "HEAL YOUR FEAR, this is the way."

The Love is sufficient.

The Ascension is near.

And the Body healed and the Spirit rejoiced.

And our power grew.

But the Dark Forces had forgotten a time would come when we would cry out for our freedom.

They were strong in the body and rich from our labor. They coveted our energy, treasured their power, and denied us our freedom and they said unto the people, "You work for us now."

But the people, awake to their glory, demanded the freedom.

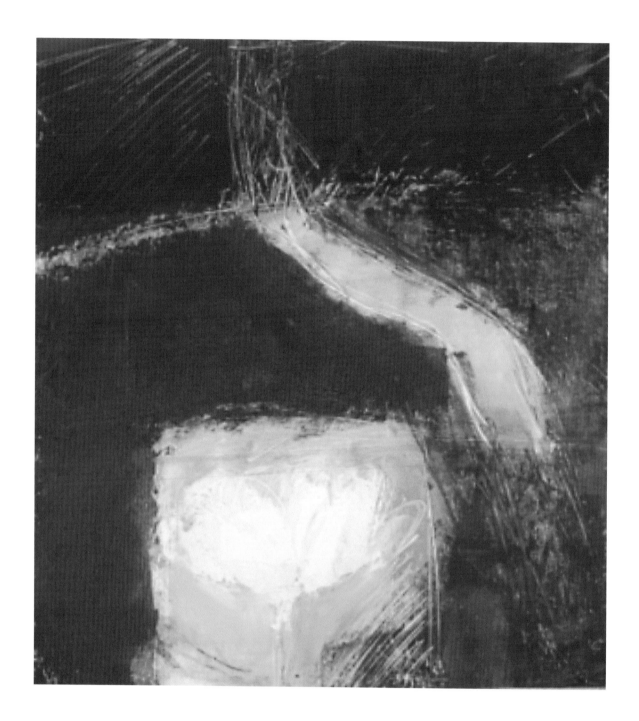

Violet and Yellow

But to this they said "No."

And the people, awake to their nature, took back their power.

And to this they screamed "Kneel!"

But the people, awake to Divinity, shone forth in glory.

So they sent the Four Horsemen.

And the plagues and the wars, the death and starvation smashed the Body and crippled the mind.

And the Body and mind, afraid of the wrath, fled back into darkness.

And Spirit thought.

What a quandary was this?

And what good could be done?

We had attained the energy.

We had achieved the awakening.

We could release kundalini.

But the Dark Forces had forgotten their purpose and would kill those that dared demand freedom.

So Spirit thought.

And Spirit called out to the omniverse and only **the strongest** responded for only they could release the Dark Forces.

And Spirit thought and from that thought the **Warriors** picked up **The Sword** and fell into the darkness.

And *Gabriel sounded her trumpet*.

And Armageddon was begun.

At the height of laughter,
the universe is flung into a
kaleidoscope of new possibilities.

Jean Houston

Part Four

Sun

And the Warriors awoke.

And the Warriors remembered.

And the Warriors stood.

And the Warriors went to the Dark Forces and said,

"The energy is sufficient."

"The Ascension will proceed."

"You **will** let the Body go."

But the Dark Forces just mocked them and said "No, we shall not" and they sent the Four Horsemen.

So the Warriors turned to the people and said, "**AWAKEN YOUR SOUL.** This is the way."

And the people said "Yes."

And the Warriors saw that the way was prepared and they smiled.

And they turned to the Dark Forces and said,

"Let the people go."

"The energy is sufficient."

"The Ascension will proceed."

But the Dark Forces just grinned and they scoffed at the warriors and spit on their faces and said "No."

So the warriors turned to the people and said "**HEAL YOUR FEAR.** This is the way."

And the people said "Yes."

And the warriors saw that the way was prepared and they smiled.

And they turned to the Dark Forces and said,

"Let the people go."

"The energy is sufficient."

"The Ascension will proceed."

But the Dark Forces just laughed and lashed out with their armies.

So the warriors turned to the people and said "**TAKE THIS SWORD**."

And with somber note, the people said "Yes."

And the warriors saw that the way was prepared and they smiled.

Golden Flowers Tree

And they turned to the Dark Forces and said,

"Let the people go."

"The energy is sufficient."

"The Ascension will proceed."

But the Dark Forces shrieked. They spewed forth vile hatred and screamed out in fear.

So the warriors turned to the people and said "**CLEANSE THIS EARTH**. Send forth your light. This is the way."

And the people, filled with joy that the time was at hand, said "Yes."

And the warriors smiled.

And The Sword cut the darkness.

And the light spread out o'r the land.

And the land burst like flames.

And the flames lit the dark.

And the darkness recoiled.

And the warriors saw that the way was prepared and they smiled.

And they opened their hands to the people.

And the people turned to the Dark Forces and said,

"Come with us."

"The energy is sufficient."

"The Ascension **will** proceed."

"Come with us."

"No old things shall stand."

And seeing that their power was gone.

And seeing they had nothing to lose.

The Dark Forces looked up.

And they saw only warmth on our faces.

And they felt only love from our hearts.

And they remembered.

And they were released.

And they saw that the way was prepared.

And they smiled.

And they turned to the warriors with honor.

And they said to the people with joy.

"The energy is sufficient."

"The love's in our hearts."

"The Ascension **will** proceed."

"God's will **now** is done."

In the beginning...

Other Books by Michael Sharp

The Book of Life:
Ascension and the Divine World Order
http://www.avatarpublication.com

A book with a message of hope.

In this book Dr. Michael Sharp explains about The Ascension, what it is about, and how (and why) it will mean profound (but positive) personal, social, political, and economic changes. Contrary to what some may think, The Ascension is not just about you, the individual, it is also about this planet (Gaia) and all of creation. The Ascension is a glorious spiritual event of creation level proportions.

In this book learn about starseeds, Indigo and Crystal Children, the nature of energy, the nature of time, the reasons behind The Ascension, our previous attempts to ascend the planet in Lemuria and Atlantis, the final struggle to transform duality and transmute negativity (i.e., the battle of Armageddon), and the glorious an inevitable conclusion to our thirty thousand year struggle. If you do not want to get caught off guard by the increasingly dramatic changes occurring on this planet or by the increases in your personal power, get serious about your personal awakening and empowerment. *Choose the Lightning Path*.

The Book of Life is available directly from Avatar Publications, Amazon.com and its international derivatives, Barnes and Noble, your local retailer, and wherever fine books are sold. Distributed by Ingram, Baker and Taylor, New Leaf, Bookworld, and others.

ISBN: 978-09735379-0-1, Retail $14.99

Dossier of the Ascension
A Practical Guide to Chakra Activation
And Kundalini Awakening
ISBN: 978-09735379-3-2
http://www.avatarpublication.com

A book with a message of power.

Learn how to activate your chakras and stay activated. Learn what to expect as you move from inefficient creator to powerful co-creator of the physical universe around you. Learn how easy it is to overcome blockage and attain the holy grail of Spiritual attainment – *full chakra awakening and safe kundalini activation.*

With the skill that only a master can bring, Michael Sharp provides all the guidance you need in order to shrug off the chains that keep you away from your spiritual power and birthright. With *The Dossier* in hand, you will quickly and efficiently throw off the fears and misconceptions that keep your chakras blocked and your kundalini in bondage.

The Dossier is a must read for anybody serious about spiritual empowerment or serious about ascension.

The Dossier of the Ascension is available directly from Avatar Publications, Amazon.com and its international derivatives, Barnes and Noble, your local retailer, and wherever fine books are sold. Distributed by Ingram, Baker and Taylor, New Leaf, Bookworld, and others.

ISBN: 978-09735379-3-2, Retail $15.99

The Book of Light:
The Nature of God, The Structure of Consciousness, And The Universe Within You

If you're looking for some answers, Dr. Michael Sharp has them for you….he promises that the book will give you a new perspective on things of a spiritual nature and he keeps his promise.... He writes about a God who loves to play, and his entertaining style fits his subject well.… I've read a lot of books on God and the meaning of life, some dull, some so dense as to be impenetrable, some apparently written in a foreign language. Often, I've felt as if I've wasted my money and time. Not so with this book. I came away with a new and fresh understanding of some ancient truths. This is an empowering book and one I highly recommend.
Sharyn McGinty - Review Coordinator - In the Library Reviews

The Book of Light
The Nature of God the Structure of Consciousness and the Universe Within You

Volume One
by Dr Michael Sharp

When you are ready to remove your chains.

The Book of Light shows you the complete truth about God, the universe, and you. Within the grounded and elegant pages of this book you will find the answers to top level theological/cosmological questions like "what is the nature of God and consciousness?", "what is the nature of the physical universe?", "what is our highest purpose?", "what is our essential nature" and more. If you ever thought that spiritual enlightenment required sacrifice, strength, or years of effort, if you think that only "the special/the chosen/the few/the evolved" get to be enlightened/saved/go to heaven, if you think ego has anything to do with enlightenment at all, think again.

Remember the simple and glorious truth of your divinity. Read *The Book of Light* and find the god within you.

The Book of Light is available directly from Avatar Publications, Amazon.com and its international derivatives, Barnes and Noble, and local retailers. Distributed by Ingram, Baker and Taylor, New Leaf, Bookworld, and others.

ISBN: 978-09738555-2-4, Retail $12.99

The Book of the Triumph of Spirit:
The New Age/New Energy Tarot System
ISBN: 978-09738555-8-6

http://www.avatarpublication.com

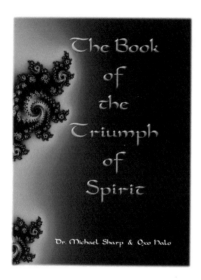

The Book of the Triumph of Spirit is a book of Tarot. In this book, Michael Sharp recovers the western tarot system as the quintessential tool for rapid enlightenment and empowerment. Several restrictive traditions are dropped and several cards are renamed in order to present the tarot in pristine purity and power.

As we remember our divinity, *The Fool* becomes *Joyful.* As we remember our purpose, *Judgment* gives way to *Redemption.* As *Initiation* progresses, *Death* is overcome.

The book includes a complete set of the revolutionary *Halo/Sharp* tarot deck. You may preview the full deck by visiting the Avatar Publications website at http://www.avatarpublication.com

ISBN: 978-09738555-8-6, Retail $29.99 (includes cards)

Printed in the United States
99357LV00001B

* 9 7 8 0 9 7 3 7 4 0 1 6 5 *